MW01644533

CONTACT INFO:
tomthebeardeddragon@gmail.com
Follow "Kelly Johnson, Author" on Facebook
Check out @tomthebeardeddragon on YouTube

ONCE UPON A

TOM

ADVENTURES OF A BEARDED DRAGON

BY KELLY JOHNSON

FOR ABE,
EMILY, KATE, ANNA, JACK, WILLIAM,
AND ALL CREATIVE KIDS.
EVERYWHERE.

TABLE OF CONTENTS

(This is the order of the book.)

Chapter 1

Who is Tom?

Best Class Pet Ever.

OK. FIRST THINGS FIRST.

A. I DON'T HAVE WINGS.

B. I CAN'T BREATHE FIRE.

C. MY DRAGON TYPE IS:

BEARDED DRAGON
(Some say Beardie)

The Teacher and Me

Mrs. Johnson

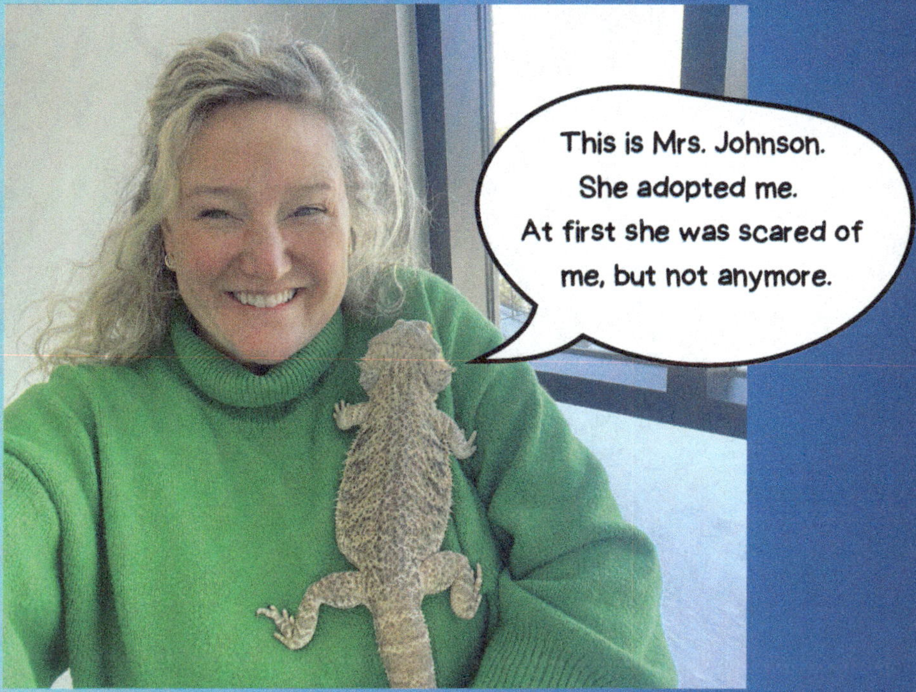

This is Mrs. Johnson.
She adopted me.
At first she was scared of
me, but not anymore.

Ahhh....
This is the
life.

I LOVE THE KIDS AT SCHOOL.
THEY LOVE ME TOO.
THEY READ WITH ME
AND I SIT CALMLY.

Being Funny

ONE DAY MRS. JOHNSON BROUGHT IN A TINY SKATEBOARD FOR ME TO RIDE ON. IT WAS THE COOLEST.

I give this skateboard 1 star out of 5. It tastes terrible.

THE NEXT DAY SHE PUT A LITTLE HAT ON ME.
THE CLASS LAUGHED.
THEY CALLED ME SANTA TOM.
I LOVE MAKING KIDS SMILE.
ESPECIALLY KIDS WHO
DON'T SMILE MUCH.

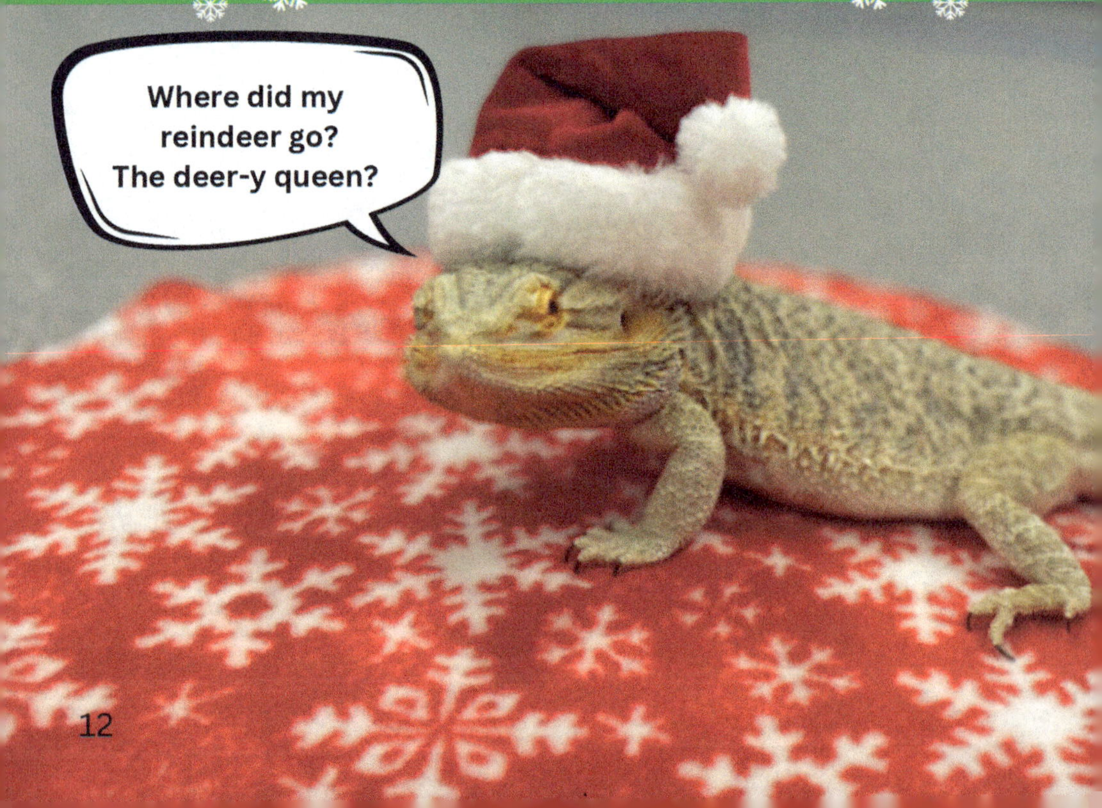

Where did my
reindeer go?
The deer-y queen?

Tom Ideas

MRS. JOHNSON STARTED COMING UP WITH DIFFERENT TOM CHARACTER IDEAS.
THIS BOOK HAS A BUNCH OF THESE CHARACTERS, AND SOME FACTS ABOUT BEARDED DRAGONS.
I HOPE THEY MAKE YOU SMILE TOO!

Chapter 2

Tom Goes to Work

Ice Cream Tom

Smooth with a little crunch- you can't go wrong with any flavor.

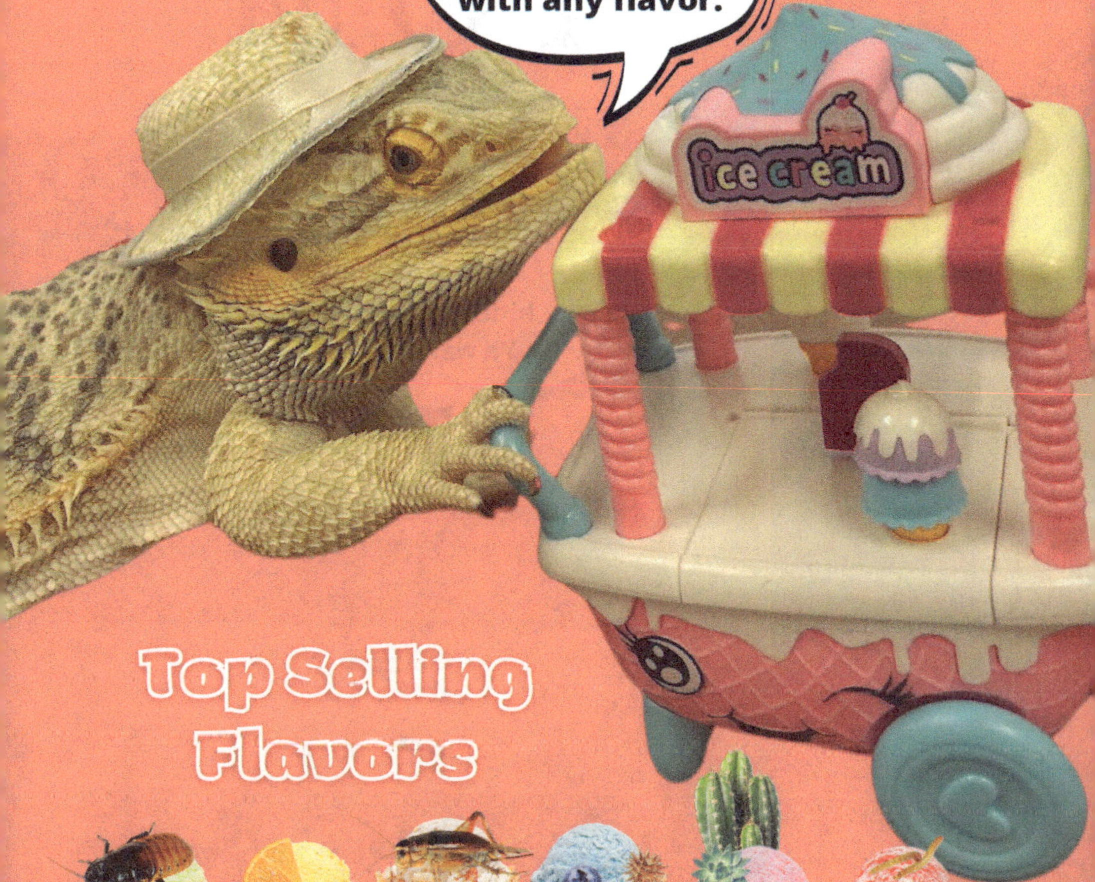

ice cream

Top Selling Flavors

Rocky Roach

Outback Orange

Cricket Crunch

Bearded Berry

Desert Dazzle

Mealworm Madness

FARMER
TOM
Hi Farmer Tom! The field mice are playing hide and seek tag. Ya wanna play?
You know I do, Petey 'ol pal!
Yahoo! We love you Tom!

WHO WILL WIN IN THIS GAME OF HIDE AND SEEK TAG?

 or

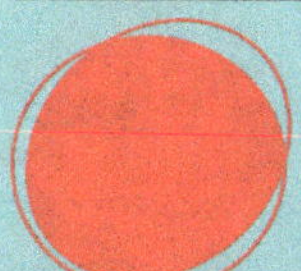 Bearded dragons can run up to nine miles per hour.

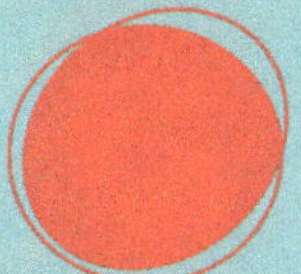 Mice can run up to eight miles per hour.

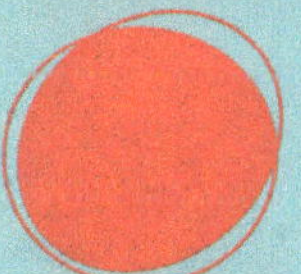 Mice can fit in a hole as small as a penny.

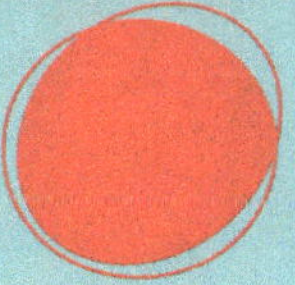 Bearded dragons can flatten themselves to the size of a pancake. (This is called "pancaking".)

CHEF TOM
Are you a
HANGRY
dragon?
Dinner. Is. Served.
Don't forget Tom's
dragon fruit salad for desert!

SUSHI TOM

FAMOUS DRAGON ROLLS

Wa-sa-bee dude?

VISIT TOM'S SUCHI RESTURANT TODAY!

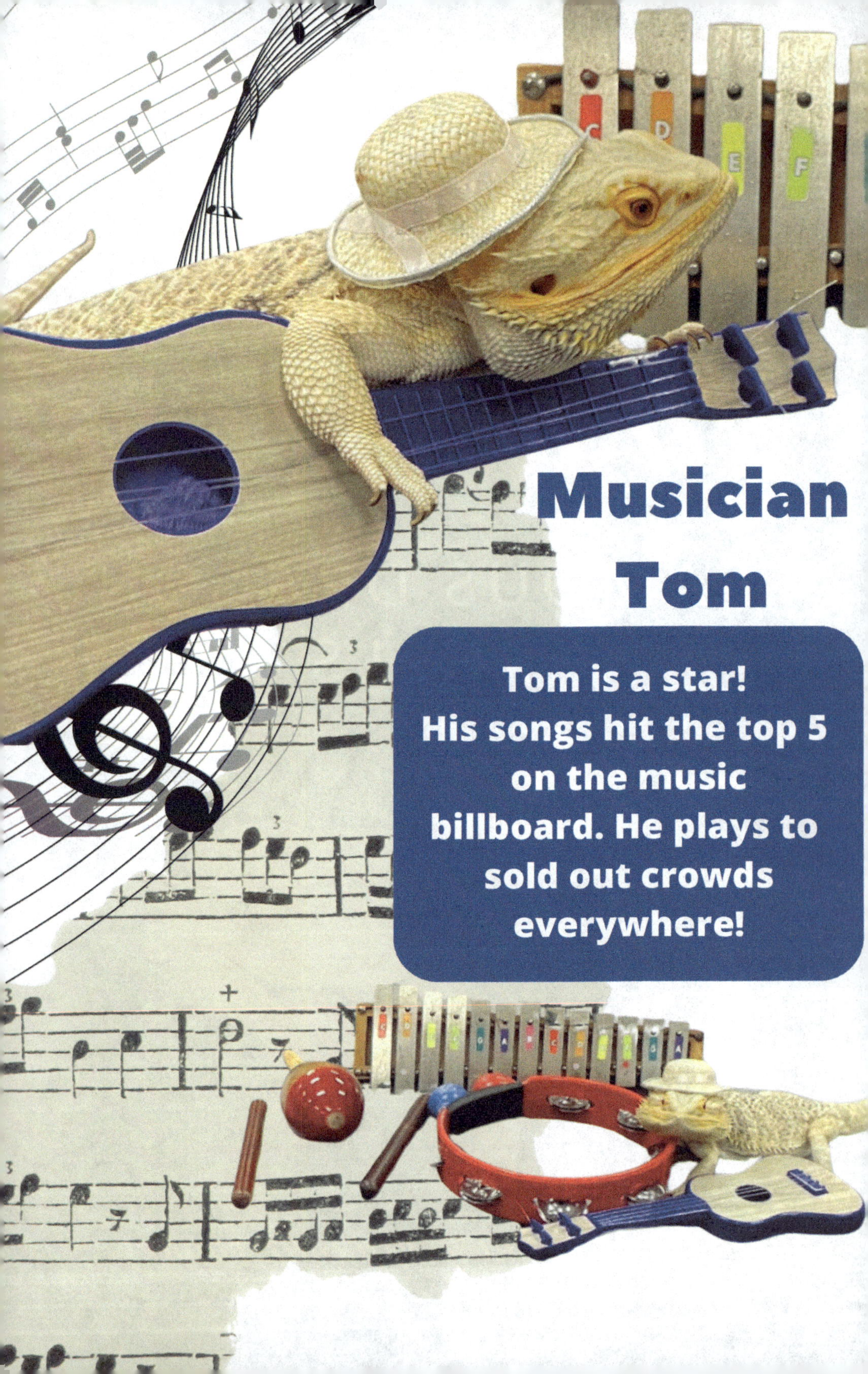

Musician
Tom
Tom is a star!
His songs hit the top 5
on the music
billboard. He plays to
sold out crowds
everywhere!

BILLBOARD

TOP 5

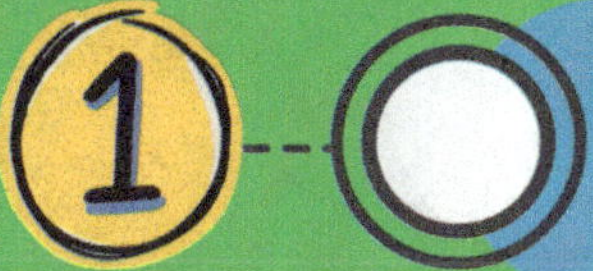

THE LIZARD AND I

Written and Performed by: Tom

TOM, THE MAGIC DRAGON

Written and Performed by: Tom

THIS DRAGON'S ON FIRE

Written and Performed by: Tom

THE TOM TOM SONG

Written and Performed by: Tom

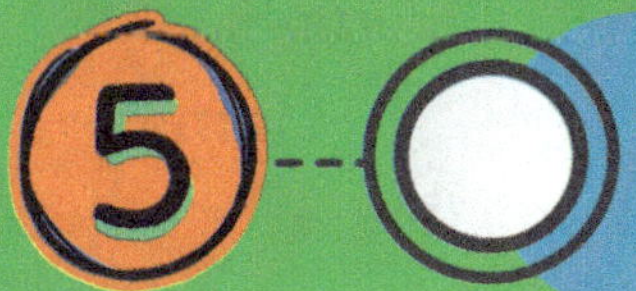

5 LITTLE DRAGONS JUMPIN' OUT DA CAGE

Written and Performed by: Tom

Get Poppin' Y'all

"Much better than dog food"
-Pup

TOM'S HAPPY CUSTOMERS

"Me like."
-Llama

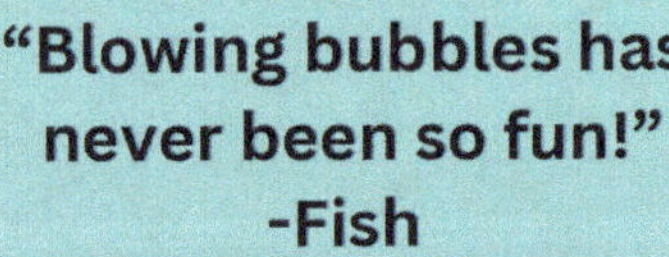

"Blowing bubbles has never been so fun!"
-Fish

Myth or Fact?

If you swallow your gum, will it stay in your stomach for 7 years?

MYTH.

Tree Farm TOM

WANNA GET FESTIVE? TOM CAN HELP.

The Tallest Tree

If you stacked up
4 Toms
(nose to tail)
you'd have the
height of an
average
Christmas tree.
The tallest
recorded
Christmas tree
was in Seattle,
Washington, in
1950.
It was 120 Toms
tall!
That is 221 feet!
It would take
a lot of lights
and ornaments
to decorate
that tree!

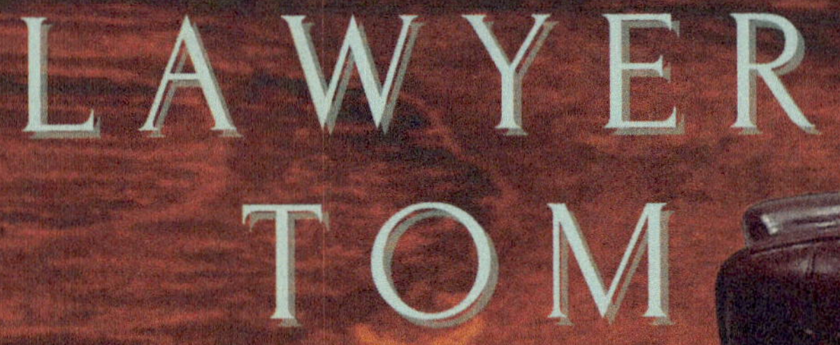

Not Guilty?
Not a Problem.

Attorney Tommy is fierce. He won my case in 15 seconds by staring at the jury.

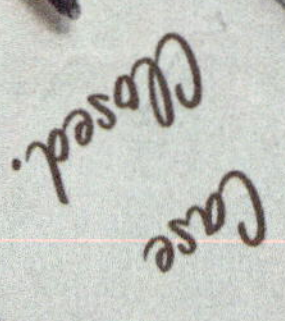

A Fierce Dragon for Justice.

DR. TOM MD.

Now, Francine, let's take a deep breath. And please, no coughing out hair balls this time.

You got it, Doctor T.

A bearded dragon's heart beats 40 to 90 times per minute. Francine here has a heartbeat of 160 to 200 beats per minute.

Pilot Tom

Hello
ladies and gentlemen.
This is Captain Tom speaking.
We're now flying over Australia.
Look closely.
You may see some
of my family.

Bearded dragons are from Australia.

They live in

deserts,

woodlands

and savannahs.

Can you find 10 Toms?
Answers on page 142.

Today's cloud cover includes bunnies, hearts, elephants, and a fire breathing dragon.
Beardy Airlines

TOM'S LENGTH

Tom measures a whopping 21 inches from the tip of his nose to the end of his tail.

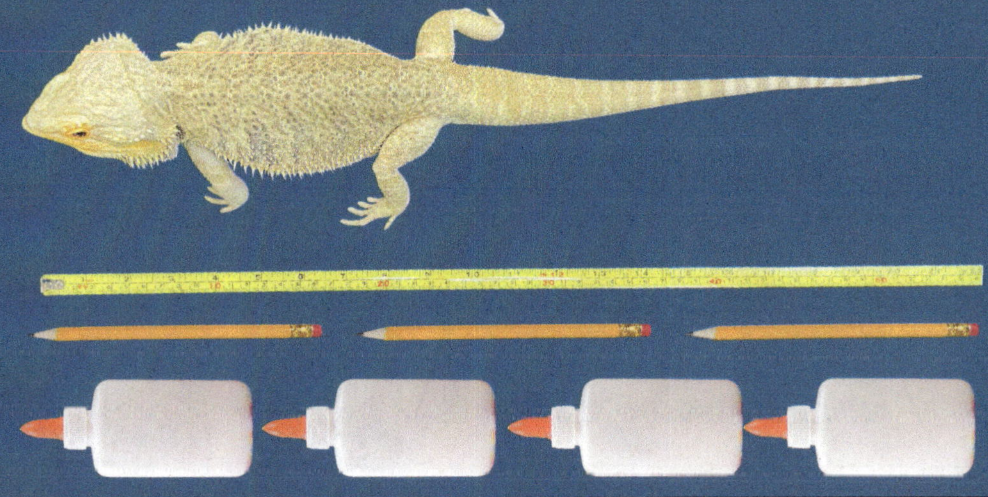

21 inches is about the length of 3 pencils or 4 glue bottles lined up.
Tom's tail is more than half of his length, measuring 11.5 inches!

FOOD TRUCK TOM

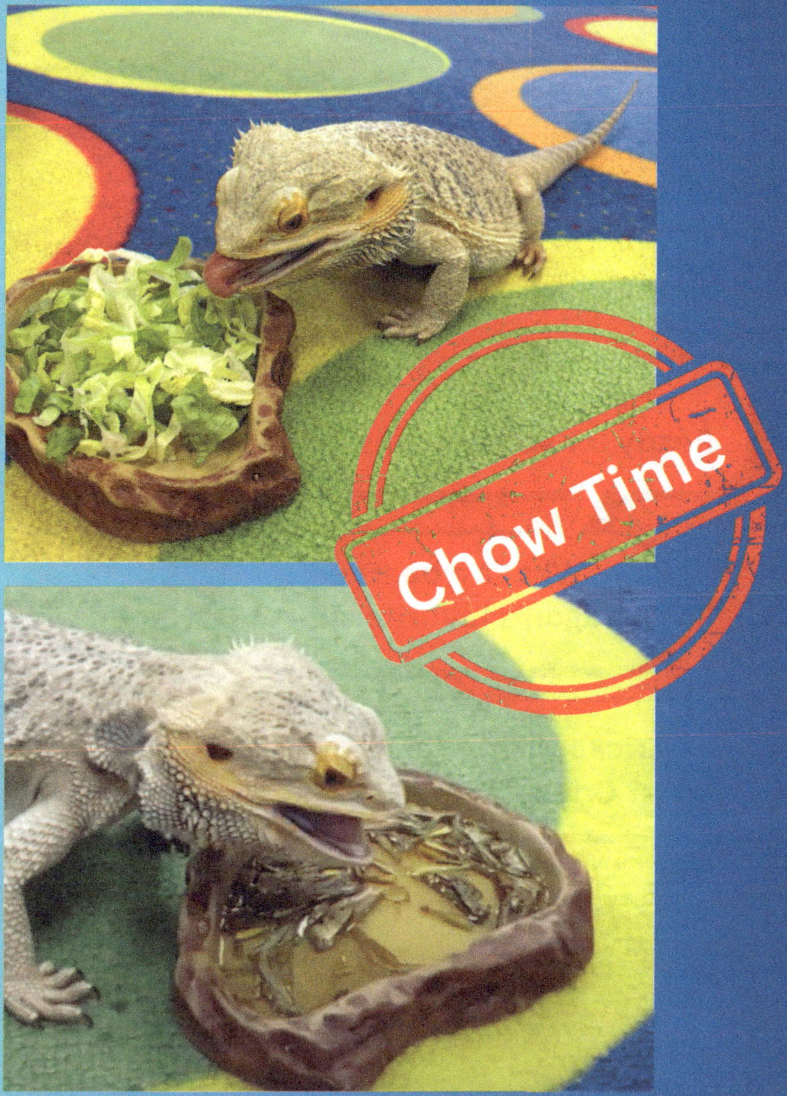

BEARDED DRAGONS LIKE TO EAT

- LIVE MEALWORMS
- CRICKETS
- VEGETABLES
- FRUITS
- HORNWORMS

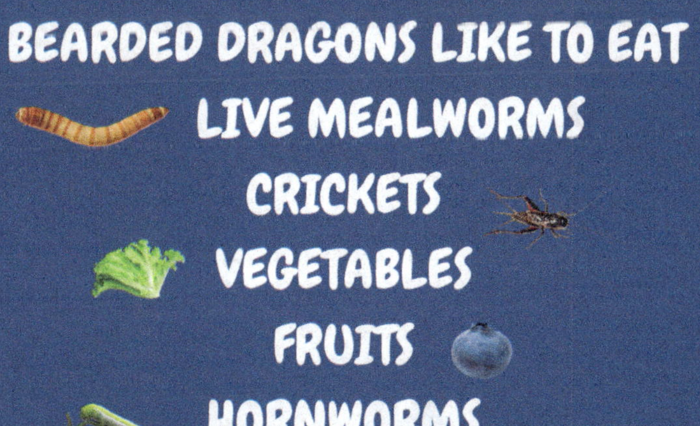

APPLAUSE
TOM COMEDY
Hey everybody.
Ready for some laughs?
What's a bearded dragon's favorite sport?
Cricket.
Get it? Cricket?
Booooo!
HA HA HA HA HA HA HA HA HA HA HA HA

More Bearded Dragon Jokes

What kind of tiles can't you stick on walls?

Rep-tiles.

What do lizards like to eat with their hamburgers?

French flies.

Tell me Einstein. Why aren't humans with beards called "Bearded Humans"?
Ze answer lies in ze universe my boy.
Scientist Tom

Parts of a Bearded Dragon

(This is called the anatomy of the bearded dragon.)

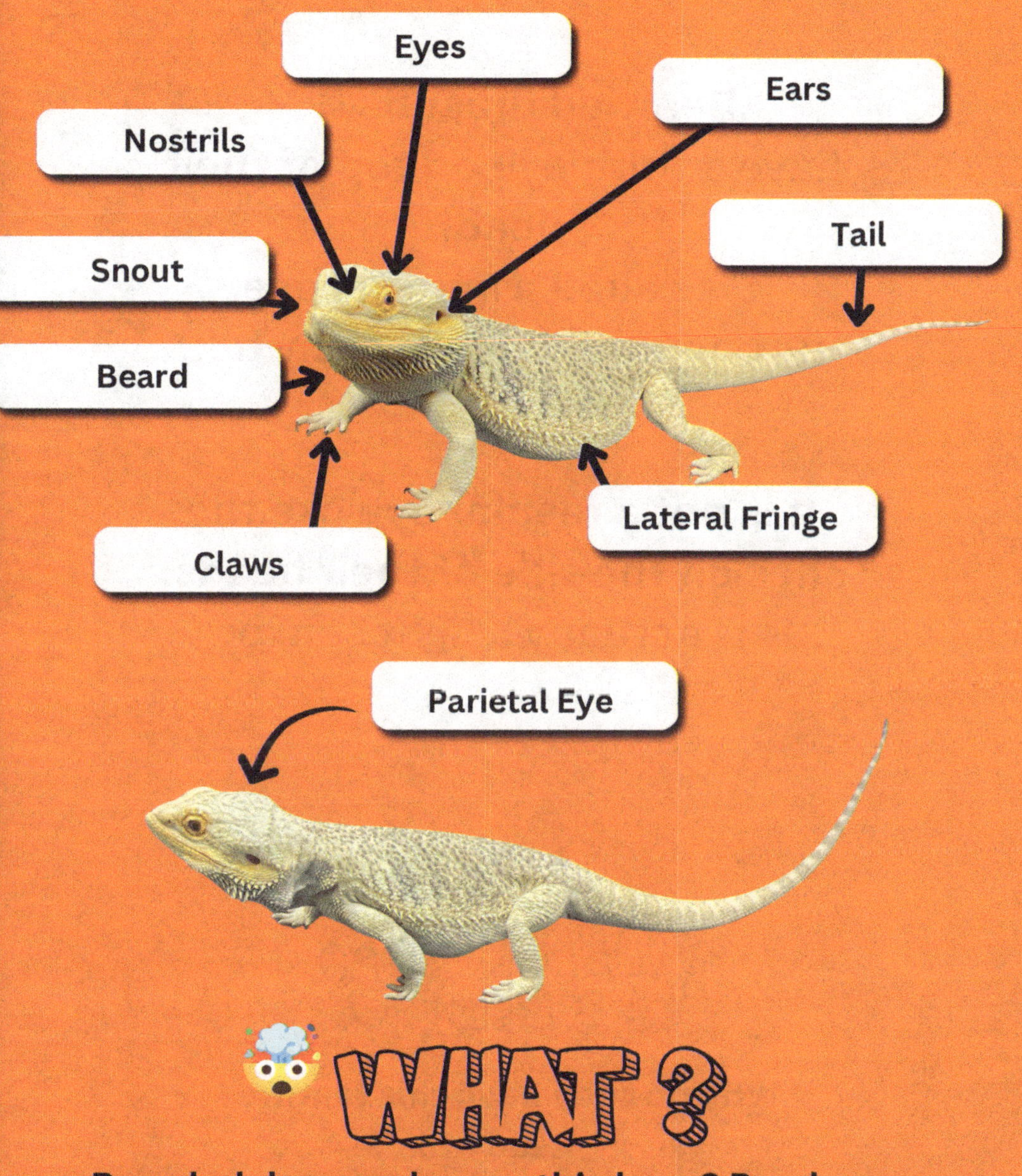

Bearded dragons have a third eye? Read on.

Bearded dragons DO have a third eye on top of their head! It is called a parietal eye. (Pronounced pur-eye-uh-tul.)

It is not a regular eye like the ones on the side of their heads. Is is actually a light sensor.

Why do they have this feature? Read on!

Attacked From Above

Beardies third eye on top of their head detects shadows. If a bird swoops overhead to eat it, the beardie will sense the shadow and hide!

Treat Yourself At Tom's Salon

No beard? Tom styles mustaches and goatees as well.

AUTHOR TOM

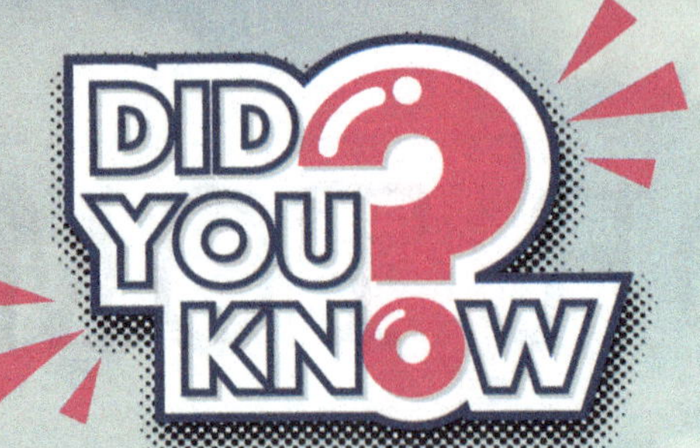

...there are exotic pet vets? They treat reptile patients, like Tom.

Veterinarian TOM

A Mystery. (True story!)

Tom had a black scale near his mouth.
We were very worried.
We brought him to an exotic pet vet.
The vet scraped off the scale and put it under a microscope.
Was is deadly? Was he sick?
What did the vet find?

Mystery Solved.

The answer?
A blueberry.

Tom had eaten blueberries, and
part of the berry had
stuck to his face and dried.
Tom was gonna be A.O.K.
Phew!
Everyone at the clinic fell in love with Tom.

CITY DRAGON
TOM

I hope traffic isn't too bad today. I've got a lot of meetings and can't get "dragon" behind schedule!

DRIVER LICENSE

Tommy Boy
BEARDY-346681011
Length: 21 inches
Eyes: Hazel

Tommy Boy

Tom Filters

More Tom Filters...
...'Cause Why Not?

Artist Tom Ross
Blue
Red-Violet
"Cat"
"Cloud"
"Apple"
Tom Ross is an absolute genius. Every artist should admire his work.

Who sees color the best?

A. HUMANS

B. DOGS

C. REPTILES

Humans have three types of color receptors in their eyes. Most reptiles have four types of color receptors. Dogs can only see shades of some colors:
blue, yellow, brown, and gray.

Answer: C

SOLVING PROBLEMS IT'S...

ENGINEER TOM

Ummm,
A little help here
Tommy? I seem to
have rolled myself
into a problem.

Which simple machine should Engineer Tom use?

"Let me hear you make some NOISE!!!"
-DJ Jazzy T

Hey kids! This ain't no chore!
Let's hit the dance floor!
Now it's your chance!
Let's do the beardie dance!

DETECTIVE TOM

Detective Tom here.
Help me crack this case!

1) Match the footprints with the animals below.

2) A treasure box has been stolen!

Catch the animal with these prints: →

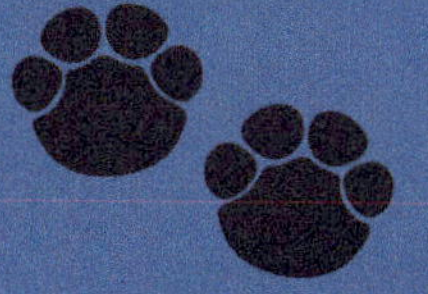

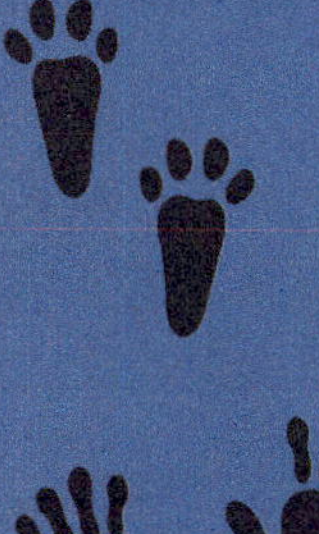

Rabbit

Monkey

Reindeer

Elephant

Penguin

Polar Bear

Turkey

Answers on page 143.

MAGICIAN
TOM

Making a rabbit appear is a LOT more difficult than it looks.

<u>Where's My Rabbit?</u>

A Poem - By Tom

Oops!
Where's my rabbit?
I made a gorilla appear?!
And now a zebra,
What's going on here?

Some chicks?
A dog in a mushroom hat?
A cat in a sweater?
I did *not* expect that.

Okay.
This trick has gotten out of hand.
This baby otter is not what I
planned.

I guess sometimes
Magic isn't so clear.
May your life be filled
with fun surprises
this year.

Magician Tom

Ssssimply the bessst.

Cute and furry.

SNAKE

HAMSTER

BEST PET CHOICE?

Yahoo!!! Yay!!!

BEARDED DRAGON FOR THE WIN!

BIRD

I'm the obvious winner.

Fish are friends.

FISH

BEARDED DRAGONS ARE AWESOME PETS BECAUSE...

MOST KIDS AREN'T ALLERGIC TO THEM.

THEY DON'T HAVE MESSY BEDDING.

THEIR FOOD ISN'T VERY EXPENSIVE.

THEIR CAGE DOESN'T SMELL BAD.

THEY BITE VERY RARELY.
(TOM HAS NEVER BITTEN ANYONE.)

OH, AND WE'RE QUIET.
EXCEPT RIGHT NOW.
BECAUSE I'M TALKING TO YOU.
BUT QUIETLY.

THEY'RE FRIENDLY, AND CUTE.

The Students and Me

I LOVE ALL OF THE KIDS AT THE SCHOOL.
THEY HELP TAKE CARE OF ME.
THEY TAKE TURNS FEEDING ME BLUEBERRIES, SALAD AND MEALWORMS.

IF A STUDENT WANTS TO PET ME, BUT FEELS NERVOUS TO USE THEIR HAND, THEY CAN USE A SOFT TOOTHBRUSH INSTEAD.

Baby Beardies

Baby bearded dragons are called hatchlings. They grow from 3 inches to 9 inches in the first two months of their lives.

3 inches is like 3 quarters in a row*.

9 inches is like a large banana*.

*Not to scale on this page.

Chapter 3

Tom Plays Sports

PICKLEBALL TOM

Pickleball has nothing to do with Pickles.
It was named after the inventor's dog, Pickles.
Tom is hoping a new sport might be named
after him one day.

BOXING TOM

There are over 300 breeds of dogs. Pork Chop is called a boxer dog. There are eight species of bearded dragons. Tom is a central bearded dragon.

Bring it on, Pork Chop!

Nothin'
but net.

BASKETBALL TOM

TAIL KICK

BACK FOOT KICK

FRONT FOOT KICK

GOALIE SAVE!

Tommy SHOOTS...

The crowd goes wild!

...and SCORES!

Bearded dragons whip their tails around for defense.

DART TOM

Big Fish: What they call the highest possible score you can get throwing darts. (170 points with 3 darts).
Little Fish: When you get 130 points with 3 darts. Tom here is just hoping for a minnow.

POOL TOM
Sinking shots all day long. That's just how I roll.
CRASH!

BASEBALL TOM

I may not *breathe* fire, but I can really "throw the heat".

DRAGONS

MONSTERS

Top Secret

TOM CAN'T THROW A KNUCKLEBALL. BEARDED DRAGONS DON'T HAVE KNUCKLES.

Game Winning Catch!

Tommy leaps!
He catches the ball!
The crowd goes wild.
The Bearded Dragons win the game!

Bearded dragons *can* jump about a foot and a half in the air. But they don't do it very often.

Cube Master Tom

The original cube was called a "Magic Cube".

"Speed cubing" sporting events are held all around the world.

There are many sizes and colors of cubes.

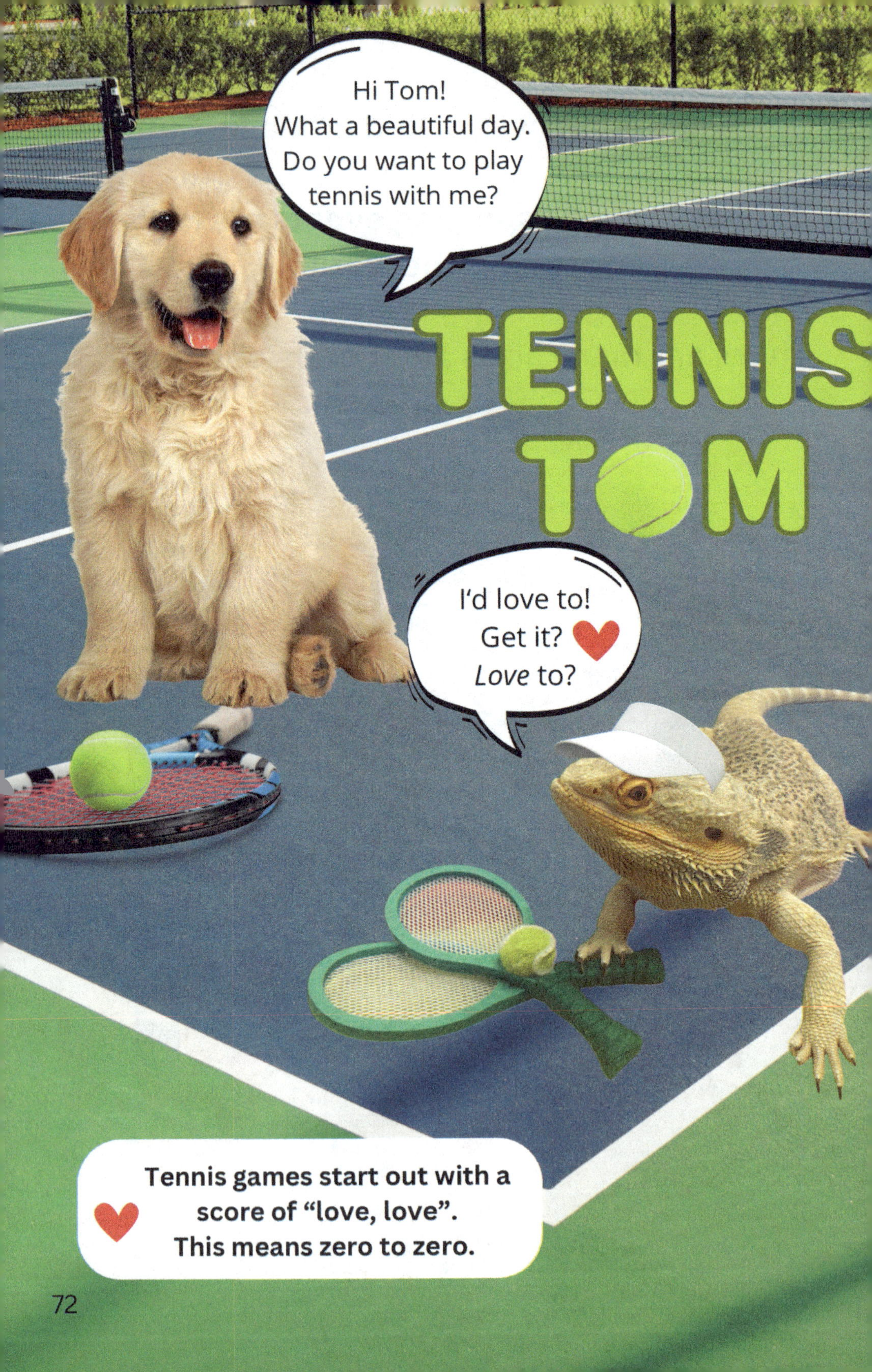
Hi Tom!
What a beautiful day.
Do you want to play
tennis with me?
TENNIS
TOM
I'd love to!
Get it?
Love to?
Tennis games start out with a
score of "love, love".
This means zero to zero.

FOOTBALL TOM

We don't stand a chance against this dragon.

First and ten, let's do it again! Push through the line, it's touchdown time!

WOLVES

DRAGONS

SKATER TOM
DUDE. I CAN DO SOME SICK TRICKS ON MY BOARD*.
*TRANSLATION:
DUDE=HEY BUDDY
SICK=AWESOME
TRICKS=MOVES
BOARD=SKATEBOARD
BEARDIES USE THEIR TAILS TO BALANCE THEMSELVES.
DO YOU THINK TOM CAN BALANCE ON THE SKATEBOARD?

SKATEBOARDING WAS INVENTED BY SURFERS WHO WANTED TO "SURF" ON DRY LAND. TOM DREAMS OF SURFING ON WATER.

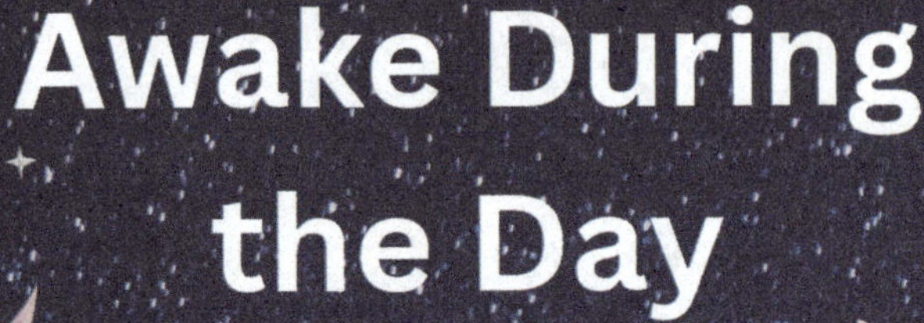

Awake During the Day

I SLEEP AT NIGHT WHEN THE KIDS ARE AT HOME. THAT MEANS I AM DIURNAL (DIE-ER-NAL), NOT NOCTURNAL. I WAKE UP WHEN THE KIDS ARIVE AT SCHOOL.

I GREET THEM BY BLINKING.

PROPS

MRS. JOHNSON GETS MY PROPS (THE THINGS I HAVE IN THE PICTURES WITH ME) FROM HER KIDS' TOY BINS, GOODWILL, AND TOY STORES. MY COSTUMES ARE OFTEN DOLL CLOTHING OR SMALL DOG OUTFITS.

Chapter 4

Tom is an Animal

Butterfly Tom

What a sweet little dragon!
Why was the bee's hair so sticky?
HONEY BEE TOM
Because he used a honey-comb!
Bearded dragons can hiss an puff up when threatened, like how a bee stings when it feels threatened.

UNICORN TOM

Don't stop....believin'

And you thought we didn't exist...

Cuteness Alert!

Baby beardies = Hatchlings
Baby dogs = Puppies
Baby cats = Kittens
Baby unicorns = Sparkles

LOBSTER TOM

Crabs, lobster, crayfish, and shrimp are all considered shellfish. Bearded dragons (although Tom likely fooled you), are not.

FOX TOM

Foxes are predators of Bearded Dragons!

Foxes can hear a mouse squeak from 100 feet away, while bearded dragons can only hear sounds from a few feet away.

SLOTH
TOM
Wheee! Yahoo!
I'm blending in quite nicely, don't you agree?
I know a bearded dragon when I see one, bub.

Sloths VS Bearded Dragons

Sloths	Bearded Dragons
About once a week sloths climb down from their tree, and poop up to 1/3 of their body weight on the ground. This has mystified scientists for ages.	Hatchlings poop more often than adults. Some beardies poop every day, every few days, or once a week. Sometimes when Tom needs to poop we give him a warm bath and tummy rub.

Bath Time for Tommy Boy

HERE I AM IN THE TUB.
THE KIDS GIVE ME TOYS TO PLAY WITH.
MY BATH LASTS 15 MINUTES.
THE WATER IS ROOM TEMPERATURE
(NOT TOO COLD AND NOT TOO HOT).
REPTILES LIKE ME ACTUALLY DRINK WATER THROUGH
OUR BODY. THAT MEANS I'M NOT JUST BATHING,
I'M ABSORBING WATER TOO!

I love to be wrapped up like a little burrito dragon.
Bath Time
TOM
Rubber Ducky you're the one. You make bath time so much fun...
SINGIN' IN THE TUB

Taking Good Care of Me

I DON'T MIND GETTING MY PICTURE TAKEN. MRS. JOHNSON IS SUPER CAREFUL WITH ME. SHE MAKES SURE I STAY WARM AND NEVER BENDS MY ARMS OR LEGS IN HARMFUL POSITIONS. EVERY PICTURE YOU SEE IN THIS BOOK WAS TAKEN WITH CARE.

Basking and Gaping

Bearded dragons don't sweat. When we bask and get warm, sometimes we "gape" (pronounced like grape without the r). We open our mouths like a dog panting. It keeps our body temperature cooler. It looks like we're smiling. 🙂

Chapter 5

Tom Has Hobbies

(And Bonus Toms)

EARTH FRIENDLY

TOM

Reuse a paper bag as a hat.
Did you ever think of that?

CAMPING TOM

Did I remember to pack bug spray? Never mind. I'll just eat them.

CARVING TOM

Almost done with my mini canoe.

Ninja Tom

Blending in
is *my*
super power.

Bearded dragons can lighten or darken their skin color to match the dirt or sand in their environment.

GAMER TOM

He's online and off the hook.

CRUSHING it here bruh.
Just beat another game.
NBD (No Big Deal).

This game better not glitch, dude.
I'm wicked good at this part.
Watch me defeat this boss!

Mrs. Johnson found this Elvis statue for free on the side of the road. She brought it home and shined it up.
My guitar is from her kids' toy bin. Thanks for sharing your toys, kids!
GUITAR LESSON TOM
You're the best guitar teacher ever, Elvis.
Well thank ya Tommy. Thank ya very much.

PIGGYBACK
TOM
Faster Tommy, Faster!! I don't got all day.
Can you believe this guy?

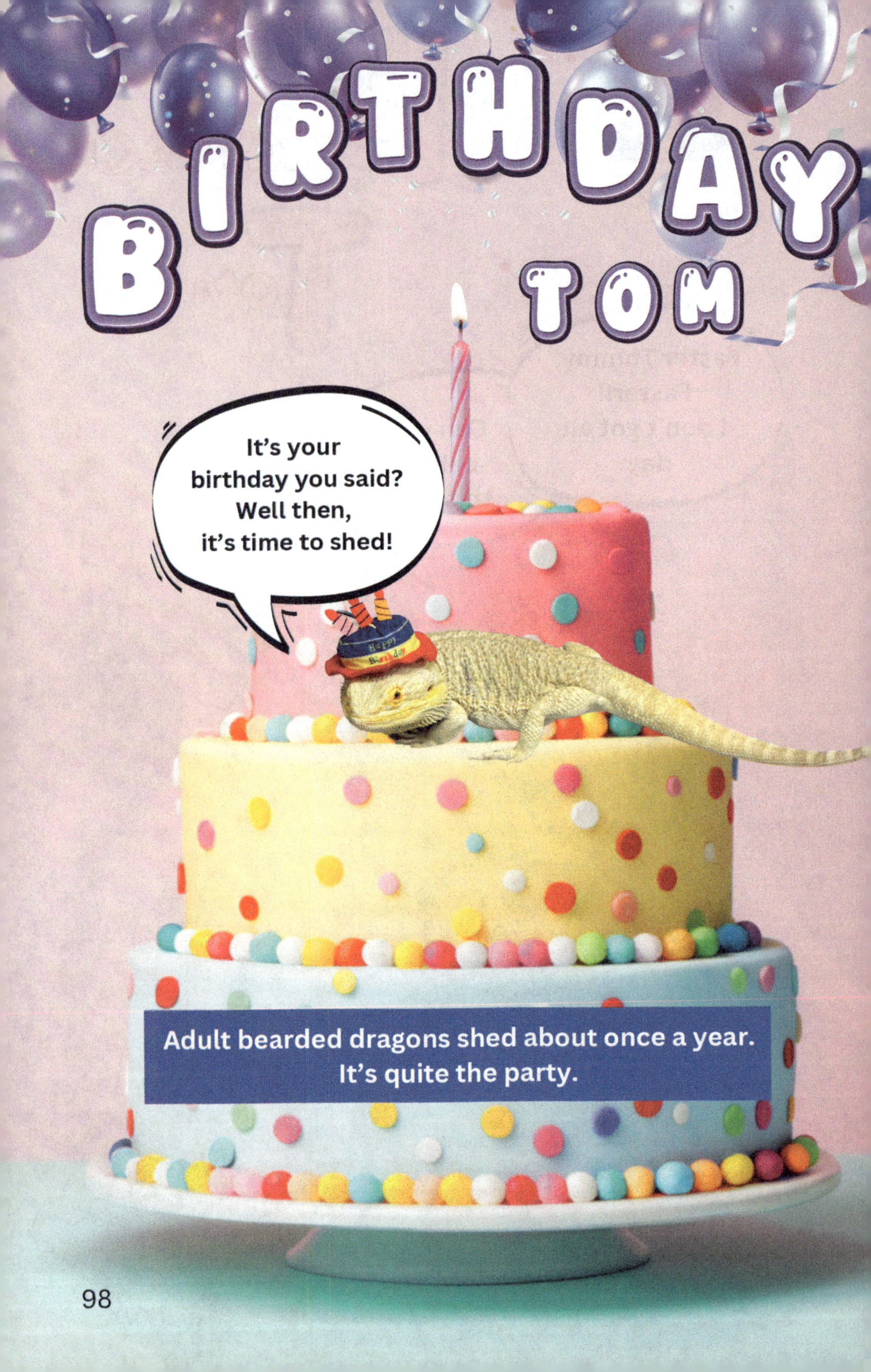

BIRTHDAY TOM

It's your birthday you said? Well then, it's time to shed!

Adult bearded dragons shed about once a year. It's quite the party.

King Tom

You must bring me the finest mealworm in all the land.

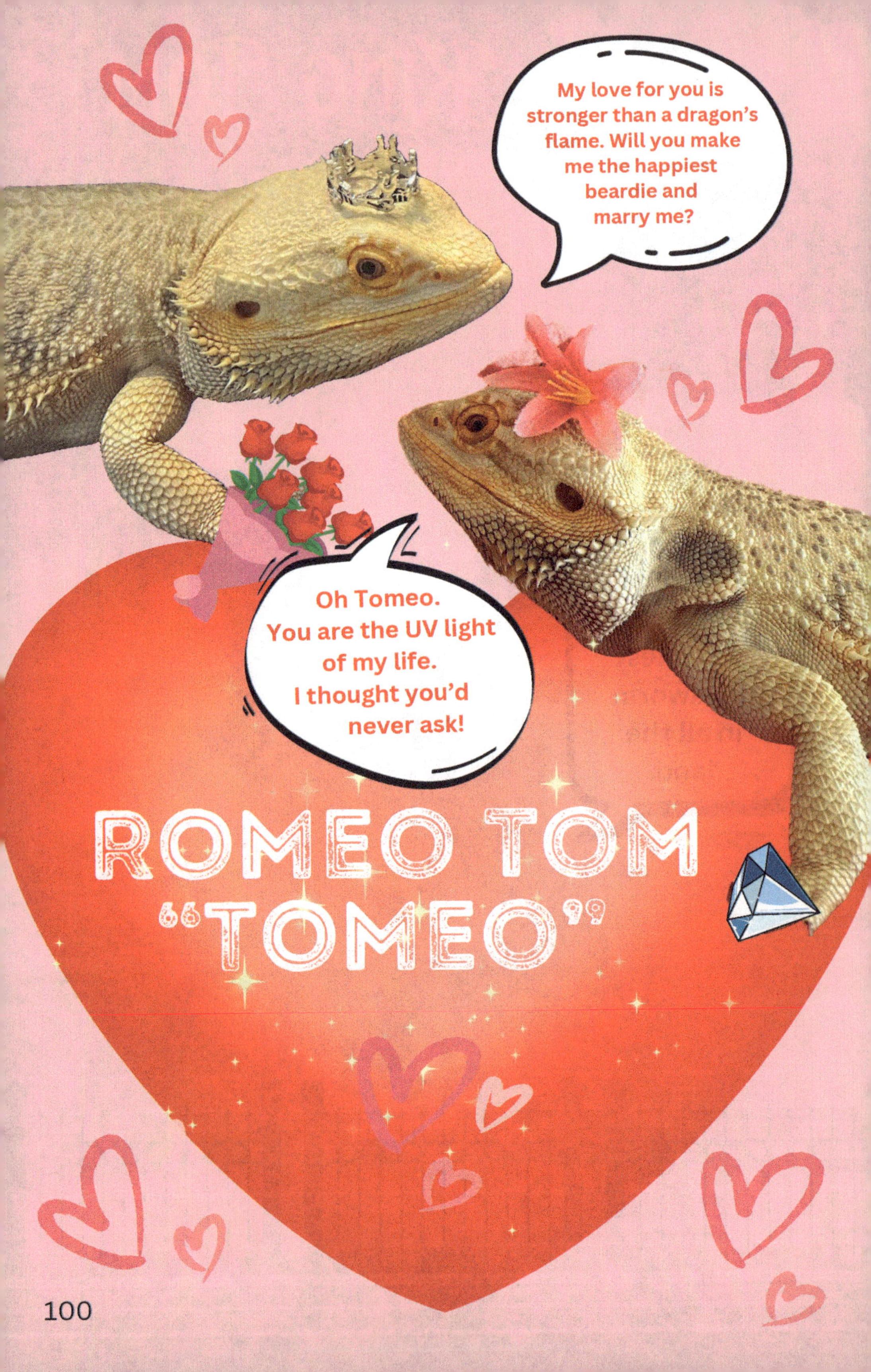
My love for you is stronger than a dragon's flame. Will you make me the happiest beardie and marry me?
Oh Tomeo. You are the UV light of my life. I thought you'd never ask!
ROMEO TOM "TOMEO"

LEPRECHAN TOM

YOU BETTER NOT CRY

YOU BETTER WATCH OUT

YOU BETTER NOT POUT
I'M TELLIN' YOU WHY...

SANTA TOM IS COMIN' TO TOWN!

Santa Tom's Reindeer Names:

Waxworm
Mealworm
Cricket
Butterworm
Roach
Hornworm
Silkworm
Superworm

The most popular day
for picnics in the
United States is
A) The 4th of July
B) Memorial Day
C) Halloween
And for desert, apple pie.
Answer: 4th of July

COZY
TOM
Snuggle Up.
I may be cold blooded, but I'm one COZY dragon.

Hanging Out
YOU ARE ROCKING THAT MATH TEST, DUDE!
I LIKE TO HANG OUT ON THE KID'S DESKS IN MY FUZZY IGLOO OR ON MY BUNKBED. I CHILL WITH THE STUDENTS WHILE THEY'RE WORKING.
IS IT SNACK TIME YET? ME HUNGRY.

Summer Tom

Tom's cage has heat lamps on top. They are set on a timer to go on at 7:00 AM and off at 7:00 PM. These lamps give warmth, and mimic the rising and setting of the sun.

The students want to take Tom out for recess to play. Even though it would be fun to see him scamper in the snow, it wouldn't be a good idea. Why not? Check out the next page.

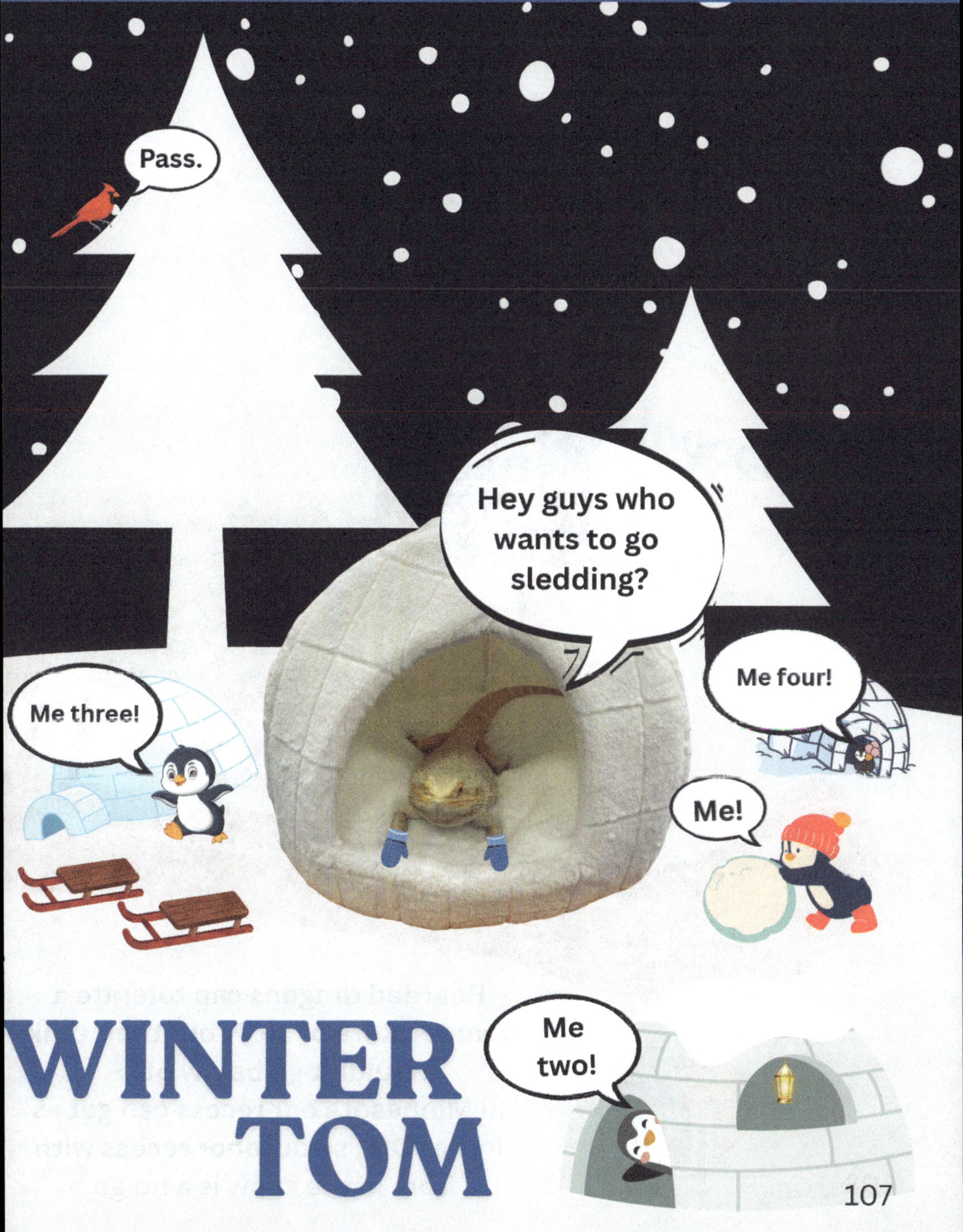

Pass.

Hey guys who wants to go sledding?

Me three!

Me four!

Me!

WINTER TOM

SLEDDING TOM

Best. Day. Ever.

Bearded dragons can tolerate a temperature of 55°F, but their tank shouldn't go below 65°F. In Minnesota our recess can get as low as 0°F, so outdoor recess with Tom in the snow is a no go.

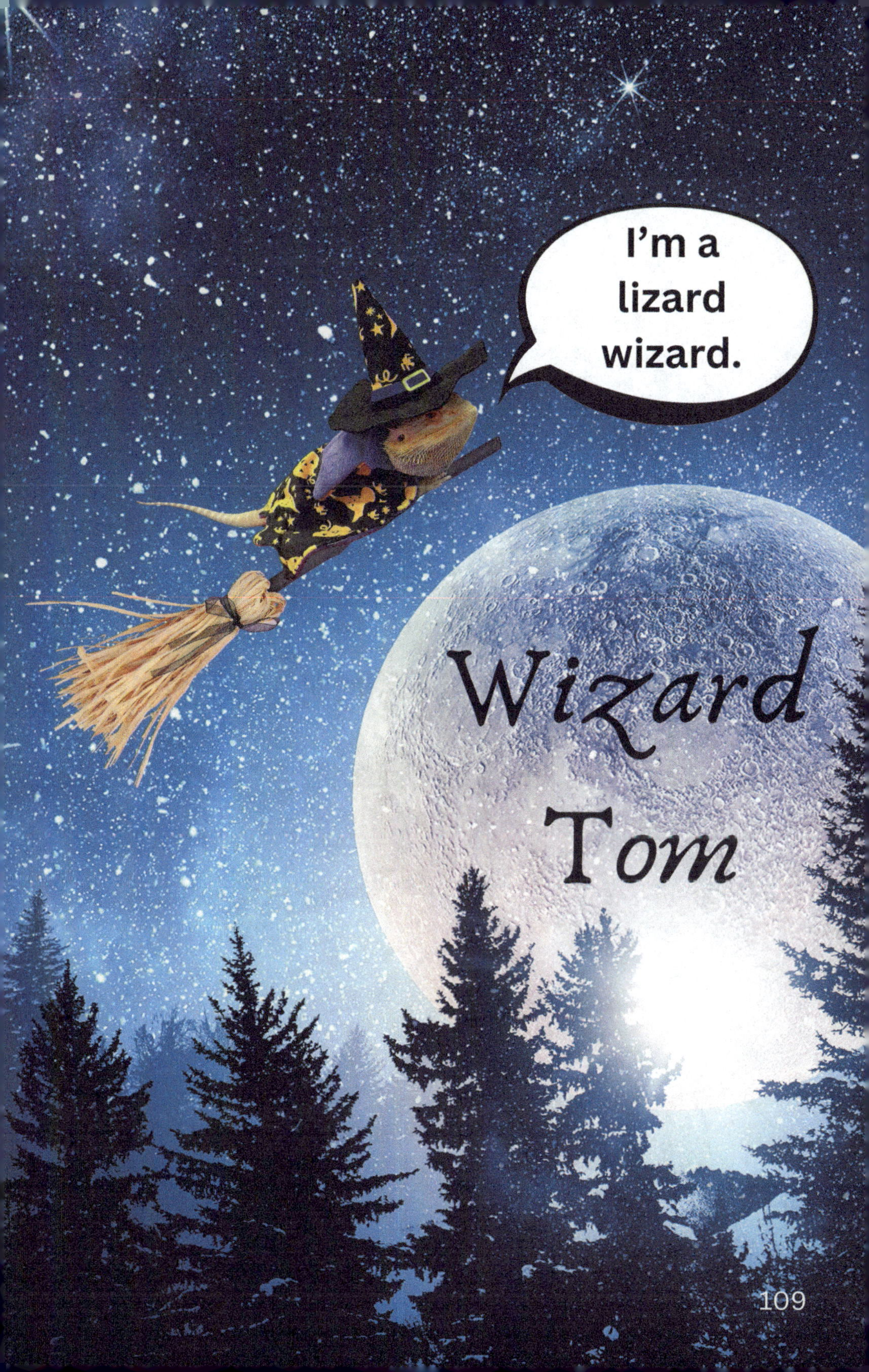

Wizard Tom

HOT

TOMALE

FIRE
BREATHING
DRAGON

INDIANA TOM
QUEST
I must find the lost city of Beard-opolis. There I shall find a blue bearded dragon!
Bearded dragons can be red, orange, yellow, tan, black, brown, gray- or the most rare: BLUE!

This cup of coffee could really use some mealworm flavoring.
COFFEE SHOP TOM

I'm going to "follow my dreams" so I'm headed back to bed. Hahaha. Congrats and goodnight!
Congratulations
GRADUATE TOM

GROCERY SHOPPING
TOM
Excuse me. Are crickets on sale today?
Shopper Tom
They sure are! 50% off today. Aisle 10.
Let's get outta here dudes!!

The Lizard of Oz

Oz

If I only had courage...

Be brave

If I only had a brain...

If I only had a heart...

If I only had a mealworm...

Chapter 6

Bloopers and Stuff

AND NOW FOR...

Tom BLOOPERS

Blooper = Embarrasing Error

Tom gets too close to the camera.

Tom BLOOPERS

Tom climbs on the props...

...and Jack.

Tom BLOOPERS

Prop problems.

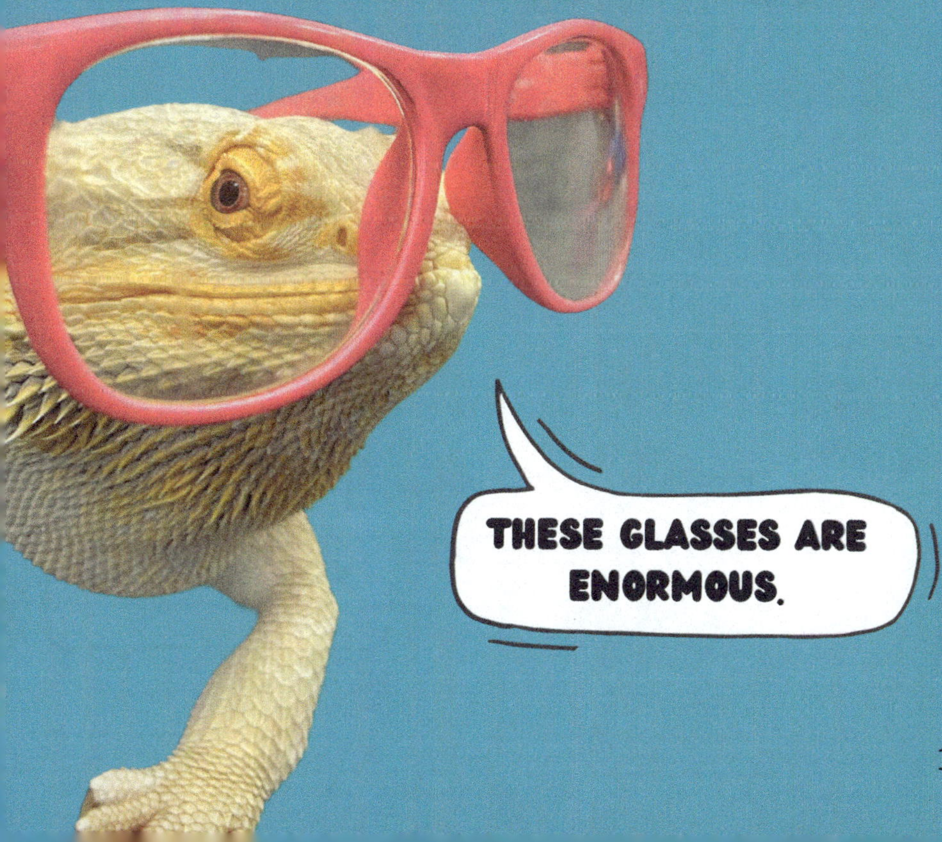

THESE GLASSES ARE ENORMOUS.

Tom BLOOPERS

Tom BLOOPERS

Tom gets an attitude.

Tom BLOOPERS

Tom gets distracted.

Take my picture?

No thanks.

I'm outta here.

Tom BLOOPERS

Tom gets suspicious.

Tom BLOOPERS

Wardrobe malfunctions.

OUR "SPIDER TOM" COSTUME DIDN'T WORK VERY WELL. THESE ARE ACTUALLY EXTRA SMALL DOG COSTUMES.

Tom BLOOPERS

Tom tries to eat the props.

Tom BLOOPERS

Tom gets silly.

What "Tom" ideas do you have?

What's kickin' little chicken?
These are called speech bubbles. They tell us what the character is saying.
Howdy-doo, kangaroo!
Sometimes speech bubbles point left like this:
Hello Jell-o!
Sometimes speech bubbles point right like this:
Yo-yo-yo Potato!
After a while, crocodile.
Later, Alligator!
Speech bubbles can be colorful,
You make me laugh, giraffe.
or black and white.
You're funny, bunny.

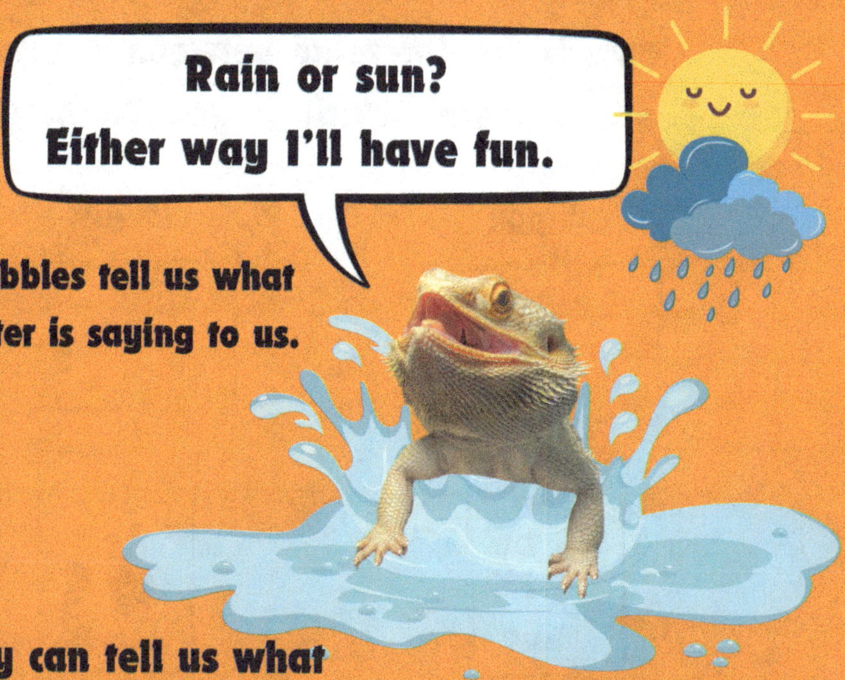

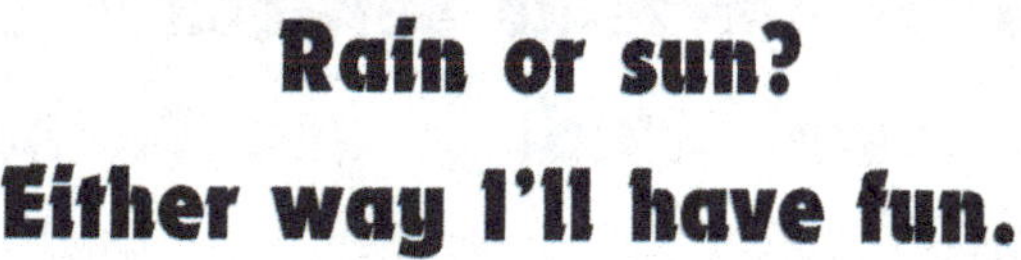

Speech bubbles tell us what the character is saying to us.

And they can tell us what characters are saying to each other.

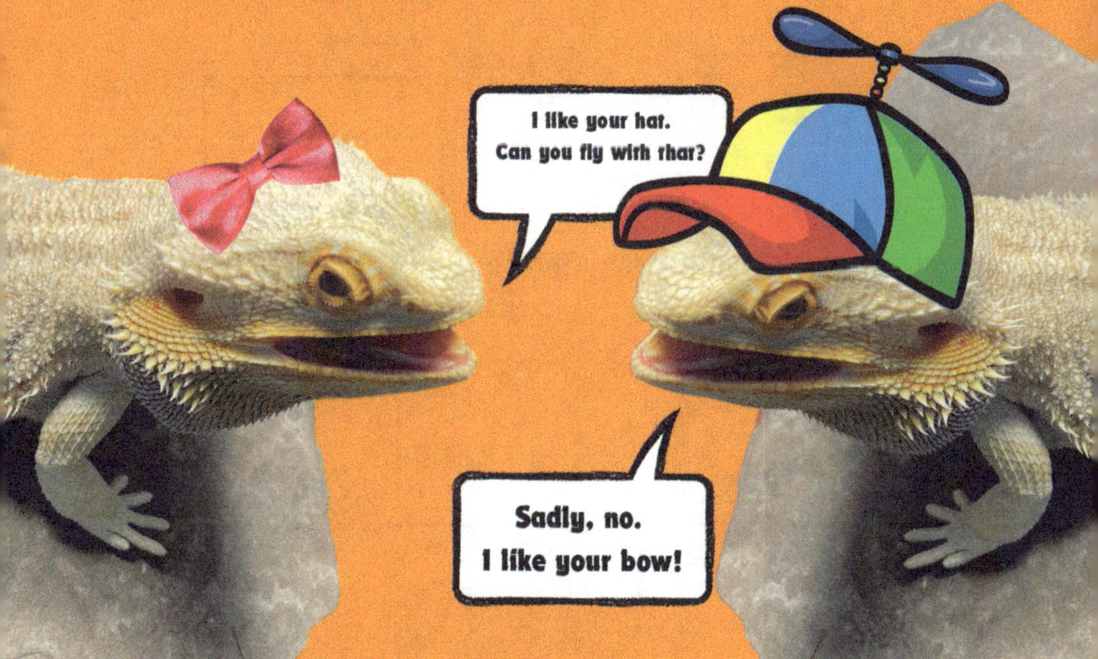

I like your hat.
Can you fly with that?

Sadly, no.
I like your bow!

Hey! That rhymes!

What is the difference between a cartoon and a photo? Which do you like better?

CARTOON VERSUS PHOTOGRAPH

This is called a thought bubble.

What is the best kind of food for a food fight?

Thought bubbles tell the reader what the character is thinking.

Why are dogs called "man's best friend?" We all know cats are <u>much</u> better.

There are usually two or three little bubbles leading to a bigger bubble.

Why *did* the chicken cross the road?

A lightbulb above their head usually means a character has an idea.

What's the big idea, Tom?

Sometimes thought bubbles tell the reader about something one character knows, but the other character doesn't.

Check out the thought bubbles on "Sloth Tom" (page 84). Does the real sloth think Tom is blending in well? How do you know?

On the next page you'll see this onomatopoeia: **PLOP**

Answer: Pool Player Tom (Page 67)

It's nice to
PLOP
down on this
bench.

Can you imagine
what the characters
are saying?

What might Tom be thinking in these pictures?

What sound could go with this picture?

How "Toms" Are Made

MRS. JOHNSON TAKES MY PICTURE WITH DIFFERENT PROPS. THEN SHE EDITS THE PICTURE TO CREATE A "TOM STORY" FOR THE KIDS.

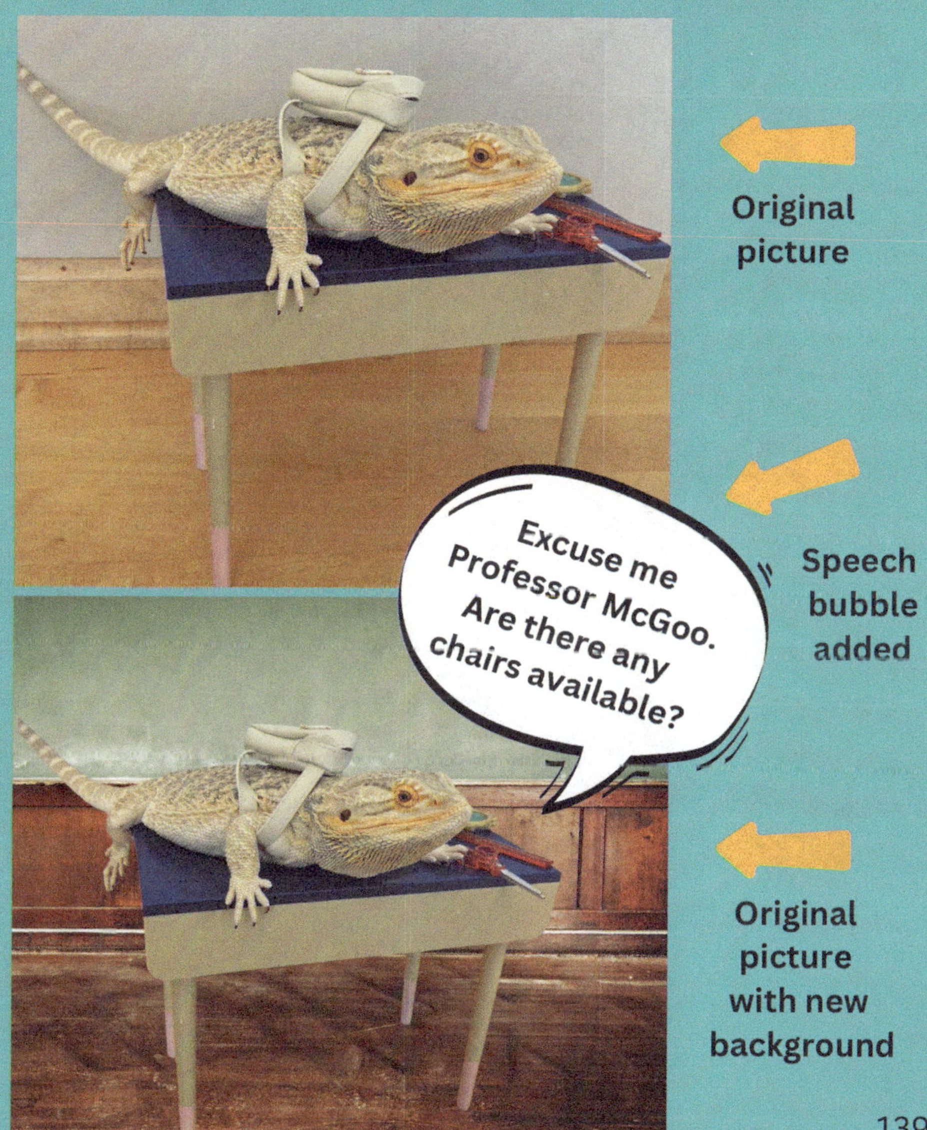

Original Picture 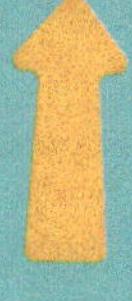

Picture with new background and embellishments 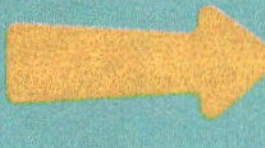

SKETCHING TOM

Did you find all 10 Toms?

How did you do matching the animals with their prints?
Which animal stole the treasure box?

Reindeer

Rabbit

Penguin

Elephant

Turkey

Did you catch me?

Polar Bear

Since I live at an elementary school I know that being a kid isn't easy. Actually, being a human of any age seems hard. I hope this book brought you a smile, and that you take time to laugh each day.
Tom
you Rock

A Note from the Author

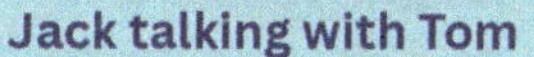

Jack talking with Tom

Anna and Tom hanging out

Hey guys! My name is Kelly Johnson and I teach at an elementary school in Minnesota. Do you know where Minnesota is? It's cold here in the winter!

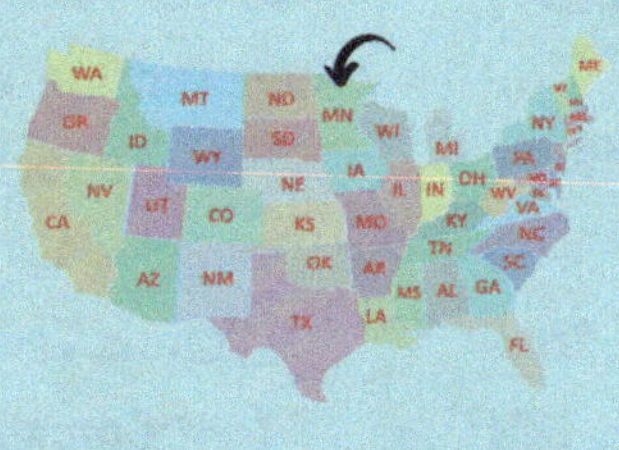

Kate playing with Tom

Several years ago my daughter Kate adopted Tom from one of her classmates. We quickly realized how amazing Tom was with kids. Kate decided it would be special for Tom to live at the school in my science classroom. That way hundreds of kids could learn about bearded dragons and how incredible they are.

Thank you to Tom's first owners, Kate, and all of the students and staff at GVP for the love and care that makes Tom.....well.....Tom!

With Love,

Kelly

(Mrs. Johnson)

Emily and Tom having fun

William feeding Tom

Index

(This is where things are listed alphabetically, with the page numbers.)

Made in United States
Orlando, FL
11 August 2025

63757529R00085